A ROMAN SOLDIER'S HANDBOOK

Alison Hawes

The author would like to thank Mr J. Brinded for his invaluable help and advice whilst researching this title.

Published 2009 by
A & C Black Publishers Ltd.
36 Soho Square, London, W1D 3QY
www.acblack.com

ISBN HB 978-1-4081-0452-1
        PB 978-1-4081-1290-8

Series consultant: Gill Matthews

This book is produced using paper that is made from wood grown in managed, sustainable forests. It is natural, renewable and recyclable. The logging and manufacturing processes conform to the environmental regulations of the country of origin.

Produced for A & C Black by Calcium.
Printed and bound in China by C&C Offset Printing Co.

All the internet addresses given in this book were correct at the time of going to press. The author and publishers regret any inconvenience caused if addresses have changed or sites have ceased to exist, but can accept no responsibility for any such changes.

Acknowledgements
The publishers would like to thank the following for their kind permission to reproduce their photographs:
Cover: Shutterstock: Mikhail Pogosov, Sue C, 9387388673; Istockphoto: Standby.
Pages: Corbis: Colin Dixon/Arcaid 15t; Dreamstime: Peter Szucs 15b, Ermine Street Guard Re-enactment Society 4, 5b, 8, 10, 20b; Istockphoto: Thomas Pullicino 11t, Tomboy2290 19b; Shutterstock: Matthew Collingwood 21t, Will Iredale 12, Javarman 19t, Verity Johnson 6, 7t, 7b, Lagui 20t, William Attard McCarthy 16, 17, Stephen Mulcahey 9t, Regien Paassen 11b, Rolandino 5t, James Steidl 9b, Sue C 13, Matka Waristka 18, Pippa West 14.

WARNING!
Children should not attempt to make or eat garum.

CONTENTS

1: SO YOU WANT TO BE A ROMAN SOLDIER?

Life as a Roman **soldier** is not easy. It is a hard, dangerous job. Only the strongest and fittest people can join the army.

"If you join up, you must stay in the army for 25 years!"

WANT TO JOIN?

The good news is that being in the army means you will be:
- well fed
- well paid
- well travelled
- well looked after when you **retire**

Do you want to be a Roman soldier? If so, you must answer yes to all these questions:

1. Are you about 18 years old? ☐
2. Are you unmarried? ☐
3. Are you a citizen of the **Roman Empire**? ☐
4. Are you willing to obey orders without question? ☐

4

You must have good eyesight. In battle you will need to see any signals that are given.

You must have good hearing. In battle, you will need to hear your orders.

You'll need to be strong. You will have lot of equipment to carry.

You'll need to be fit. There will be a lot of marching.

SPEAKING THE LANGUAGE

If you don't speak **Latin** (perhaps you are from France or Spain) you must learn it.

"All your training and orders will be in Latin."

Intente! (Attention!)

TOP TIP

If you know someone important, ask them to write a letter of recommendation for you. This will help you get into the army.

2: THE UNIFORM

Your basic uniform consists of a knee-length tunic with short sleeves and a pair of open leather boots.

WINTER CLOTHES

In winter, you will wear a long-sleeved tunic, trousers, socks, and closed boots. You'll also be given a woollen cloak to keep you warm.

HELMET

Your helmet will be made of brass or iron. Pieces on the side stick out and protect your face. Pieces on the back stick out and protect your neck.

"Tie your helmet under the chin using the leather strap."

Leather strap

BODY ARMOUR

Roman soldiers wear three different types of body armour:

Ring-mail armour: A ring-mail shirt is very heavy. Most Roman soldiers wear this type of armour.

Fish-scale armour: Fish-scale armour is made up of tiny pieces of metal sewn onto leather. **Officers** usually wear this type of armour.

Plate armour: Plate armour is made up of thin, overlapping bands of metal. Both regular soldiers and officers wear this type of armour.

"Your shirt will be made of hundreds of linked metal rings."

"A short-sleeved metal jacket is held together with hooks, laces, and straps."

TOP TIP

Remember to wear a scarf under your armour. It will stop it from digging into your neck!

3: THE WEAPONS

You can use five weapons: a sword, shield, dagger, and two throwing spears.

YOUR SWORD

The sword (gladius) is light and about 50 cm (20 in) long. It has a sharp, iron blade. It makes a good stabbing weapon. You wear it on the right side of your body, at your waist.

USING YOUR WEAPONS

- Use your sword in your right hand (even if you are left-handed). You can then stand in close formation, ready to march into battle.
- Your dagger (pugio) is even smaller than your sword. If you lose your sword in battle, use your dagger instead.
- Your shield (scutum) is curved and rectangular so:
  - it fits around your body to protect it
  - it deflects most blows

"A sword."

"Several layers of wood are glued together to make your shield strong but light."

Boss

- In battle, use your shield as a weapon. Smash the metal boss into the enemy and then stab at him with your sword.
- At the start of a battle, throw your spear (pilum) at the enemy. The metal tip of these 2 m (6.5 ft) long spears is so sharp it can pierce metal body armour.
- If a spear misses the enemy and hits the ground, it will fall apart. This means the enemy cannot throw it back at you.

"Throwing a spear."

4: TRAINING

You will go to a training camp when you first join the army. Here, you'll spend most of your time keeping fit and learning to use your weapons.

"Basic training lasts about four months."

KEEPING FIT

Most days you'll be running, marching, swimming, or wrestling.

WEAPONS TRAINING

You start your training with wooden weapons and move on to the real thing when you are skilled enough.

LONG MARCHES

Every ten days, you will go on a long march. You will march about 32 km (20 miles) each time, in full uniform and carrying your weapons and kit.

MAKING CAMP

You will share a goatskin tent with seven other soldiers. You must set up camp quickly. All camps are made the same way:
- dig a ditch
- put up a fence
- put up the tents

SIGNALS

You will be taught to recognise and obey signals given in battle. Some signals are given on a horn or trumpet. Others are given with banners called **standards**.

Horn

"Be warned! The sword, shield, and spear you train with are twice as heavy as the real ones. So you need to be strong!"

5. FIGHTING BATTLES

Once you have mastered how to use your weapons, you must then learn how to fight successfully in a battle.

BATTLE FORMATION

When you march into battle you must not march or run ahead on your own. You march into battle together, in formation. Roman soldiers win battles because they fight together, as one **unit**.

FIGHTING MACHINES

When you are attacking a **fort**, you will have to build fighting machines to help you.

"This machine is called an onager. Use it to hurl big rocks or fire stones at the enemy."

THE TORTOISE

If you need to get up close to an enemy fort, get into the tortoise formation with the soldiers next to you for protection.

"The shields protect you from arrows and rocks thrown from above."

SHEDS AND TOWERS

If you need to break into a fort, you must build special sheds and towers to help you.

6. BUILDING PROJECTS

It's hard work being a Roman soldier.
When you are not training or fighting,
you'll be given lots of building work to do.

ROAD BUILDERS

A lot of your time will be
spent building roads and
bridges. Soldiers can move
from place to place quickly
on good roads and bridges.

Good roads mean letters
from home will arrive sooner.

"Road building is
hard work. Build
them fast, but build
them to last."

TOP TIP

It helps to have a special skill, such
as being good at writing or looking
after horses. Then you won't have
to do the boring jobs, such as
guard duty or cleaning.

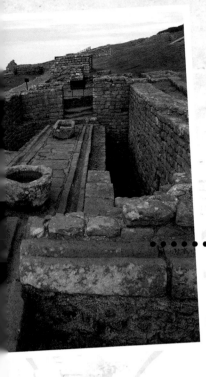

FORTS

You may also have to build a fort to live in. Forts are usually built of wood, but you may have to help rebuild one in stone. That will make it stronger and last longer. At a fort, you will sleep in a room, rather than a tent. You will share with the soldiers in your unit.

Life in a fort is better than life on the road. Each fort has its own baths, toilets, hospital, and bakery.

TOWNS

Towns are often built up around forts. You could be asked to help lay out the streets, dig a well, or build an **aqueduct** or the town walls.

"Aqueducts bring fresh, clean water from the hills to a town."

7: REWARDS AND PUNISHMENTS

Soldiers who win battles or save lives will be rewarded. You could be given money or a special medal or crown to wear. Most of the rewards go to the officers, not the regular soldiers.

HOW TO BECOME A CENTURION

A regular solider like you can become a **centurion** if you are:
- brave
- clever
- and if you work hard

"Officers wear golden crowns and medals when they are on parade."

16

As an officer, you will be paid much more than regular soldiers. You will wear a crest on your helmet and leg guards, so everyone knows you are an officer.

PUNISHMENTS

Obey orders and work hard at all times. The officers will punish you if you don't. If you are lazy, an officer might:

- hit you with his cane
- cut your food rations
- give you more work to do

But for something more serious, such as stealing, you could be beaten.

"Centurions also wear the sword and dagger on the opposite side to a regular soldier."

Cane

8. WHAT YOU WILL EAT

Roman soldiers eat well. Good food will keep you strong and healthy. What you eat depends on whether you are on the march or in a fort.

ON THE MARCH

Soldiers on the move eat dried, salted, or smoked foods. Hard biscuits, bacon, cheese, and wine will keep for a few days without going bad.

IN A FORT

You will eat a wider range of food in a fort. Forts house animals for fresh meat, and there will be fresh vegetables to eat. You will also get the chance to hunt for food.

"You may be able to hunt birds or deer or catch fish and shellfish. It depends on where your camp is."

Your daily food ration will include:
- bread
- olive oil
- meat
- wine

You need to eat a lot of bread (panis). It gives you energy. Each group of soldiers has two stones to grind wheat into flour to make bread.

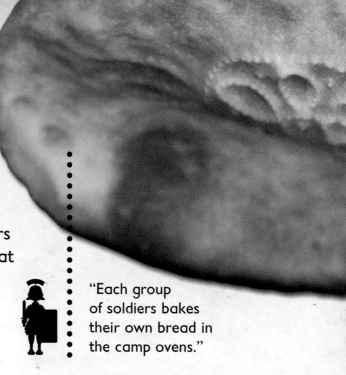

"Each group of soldiers bakes their own bread in the camp ovens."

FISH SAUCE (GARUM)

Most soldiers keep a small flask of garum in their kit. You can add this salty, fishy sauce to almost everything you eat.

Garum recipe for soldiers

You will need:
Dried herbs
Fatty fish (anchovies or sardines)
Salt
Cooking pot with a lid

1. Put a thin layer of herbs in the pot.
2. Top with a layer of fish.
3. Cover with a thick layer of salt.
4. Add more layers until the pot is full.
5. Leave the pot in a hot, sunny place.
6. Stir the mixture every day.
7. In a month, the garum should be runny and smelly. Delicious!

9: WHAT YOU WILL GET PAID

You get some money when you first join the army. After that you will earn about 300 **denarii** a year. You might get extra pay when you win a battle or when Rome gets a new **emperor**.

"A silver denarius."

SOLDIER'S EXPENSES

Most of your pay will go on your food, bedding, and uniform.

"Look after your weapons. You will have to buy new ones if you don't!"

———— Sword

SPARE CASH

You will have a bit of spare cash when you have paid for all your expenses. You can use that money for fun!

"Use some of your hard-earned money to spend an afternoon at the baths with your friends."

TOP TIP

Don't spend all your spare cash. You will need to save for retirement.

RETIREMENT

You will be given about ten years' pay when you retire. You will also get your savings from the savings fund.

DEATH

Your burial fund will pay for your funeral when you die.

GLOSSARY

aqueduct a stone structure that carries water from its source to a town

cemetery a graveyard

centurion an officer in the Roman army

denarii Roman coins

emperor the ruler of an empire

fort a well-defended place where soldiers live

Latin the language spoken by the Romans

military anything to do with the army

officers the people in charge of the regular soldiers

retire to stop doing paid work

Roman Empire all the countries and land occupied by Romans

soldier there were two kinds of Roman soldiers — legionaries and auxiliaries. This book tells you about legionary soldiers from the first century AD

standards the special banners carried by the Roman armies

unit a group

FURTHER INFORMATION

WEBSITES

BBC Roman website at:
www.bbc.co.uk/schools/romans/army.shtml

Woodlands junior school homework website at:
**www.woodlands-junior.kent.sch.uk/Homework/
  Romans.html**

BOOKS

The Roman Army by P. Connolly. Silver Burdett (1979)

The Romans in Britain by B.J. Knapp. Atlantic Europe (2004)

Avoid Being a Roman Soldier by D. Stewart. Book House (2006)

PLACES TO VISIT

Housesteads Roman Fort
Haydon Bridge, Northumberland

Vindolanda and Roman Army Museum
Hexham, Northumberland

Lunt Roman Fort
Baginton, Coventry

Roman Legionary Museum
Caerleon, Gwent

INDEX